In the Money

A Book About Banking

by Nancy Loewen * illustrated by Brad Fitzpatrick

Thanks to our advisers for their expertise, research, and advice:

Dr. Joseph Santos
Associate Professor of Economics, Department of Economics
South Dakota State University

Susan Kesselring, M.A., Literacy Educator
Rosemount–Apple Valley–Eagan (Minnesota) School District

PICTURE WINDOW BOOKS
Minneapolis, Minnesota

--Editorial Director: Carol Jones
Managing Editor: Catherine Neitge
Creative Director: Keith Griffin
Editor: Christianne Jones
Story Consultant: Terry Flaherty
Designer: Joe Anderson
Page Production: Picture Window Books
The illustrations in this book were created digitally.

Picture Window Books
5115 Excelsior Boulevard
Suite 232
Minneapolis, MN 55416
877-845-8392
www.picturewindowbooks.com

Printed in the United States of America.

**Library of Congress
Cataloging-in-Publication Data**
Loewen, Nancy, 1964-
In the money : a book about banking / by Nancy Loewen ;
illustrated by Brad Fitzpatrick.
p. cm. — (Money matters)
Includes bibliographical references and index.
ISBN 978-1-4048-1156-0 (hardcover)
1. Banks and banking—Juvenile literature.
I. Fitzpatrick, Brad, ill. II. Title. III. Money matters
(Minneapolis, Minn.)

HG1609.L64 2006
332.1—dc22   2005004063

"Good morning! Time to get up!" Mom said.

"I don't have to go to school today," David said. "It's Take Your Child to Work Day. You're going to show me what you do as a loan officer at the bank."

"That's right," Mom replied. "There's a lot to see at the bank, so get moving!"

3

"How long have banks been around? Did you have banks when you were a kid?" David asked his mom.

4

"I'm not that old!" she said with a laugh. "Banks have been around for hundreds of years. The very first banks were in ancient Mesopotamia. People used grain as money. Temples and palaces offered people safe places to store it."

In 1781, the first official bank in the United States opened in Philadelphia, Pennsylvania.

5

Employees were typing at computers or talking on the phone—sometimes both at the same time. Others were sorting through stacks of paper. In the lobby, a couple of people were loading cash into the automatic teller machine, or ATM.

"Do you want to watch the tellers?" Mom asked.

"What's a teller?" asked David. "Are they like story tellers?"

"Tellers are the people who help the customers," Mom answered.

"But sometimes we like to tell stories, too," a young woman said with a smile. "Hi, David, I'm Holly."

"Could you show David his savings account?" Mom asked Holly. "Here's his account number."

"No problem," said Holly. She typed the number into the computer.

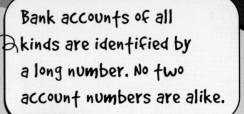

Bank accounts of all kinds are identified by a long number. No two account numbers are alike.

On the computer screen, David could see the deposits and withdrawals he had made. He also saw a small deposit that he didn't remember making.

"Where did that money come from?" he asked.

"That's the interest you earned on your account," Holly replied. "Interest is what the bank pays people to keep their money here."

"When people borrow money, they pay interest to the bank," Mom added. "Those are the two main jobs of a bank: to be a safe place for people to keep their money, and to lend money to people for big purchases."

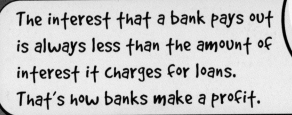

The interest that a bank pays out is always less than the amount of interest it charges for loans. That's how banks make a profit.

David sat on a stool and watched as Holly took cash and checks from customers and put them into a drawer. For every transaction, she printed out a receipt and gave it to the customer. One man cashed a check for $200. Holly counted out $20 bills so fast, her fingers were a blur.

"Wow! You could be a magician!" David exclaimed.

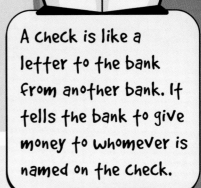

A check is like a letter to the bank from another bank. It tells the bank to give money to whomever is named on the check.

13

A woman came in with a badly torn $10 bill. Holly took the bill and gave her a crisp new one.

"What happens to that old money?" David asked.

Federal Reserve Banks are located in these cities: Boston, New York, Philadelphia, Cleveland, Richmond, Atlanta, Chicago, St. Louis, Minneapolis, Kansas City, Dallas, and San Francisco.

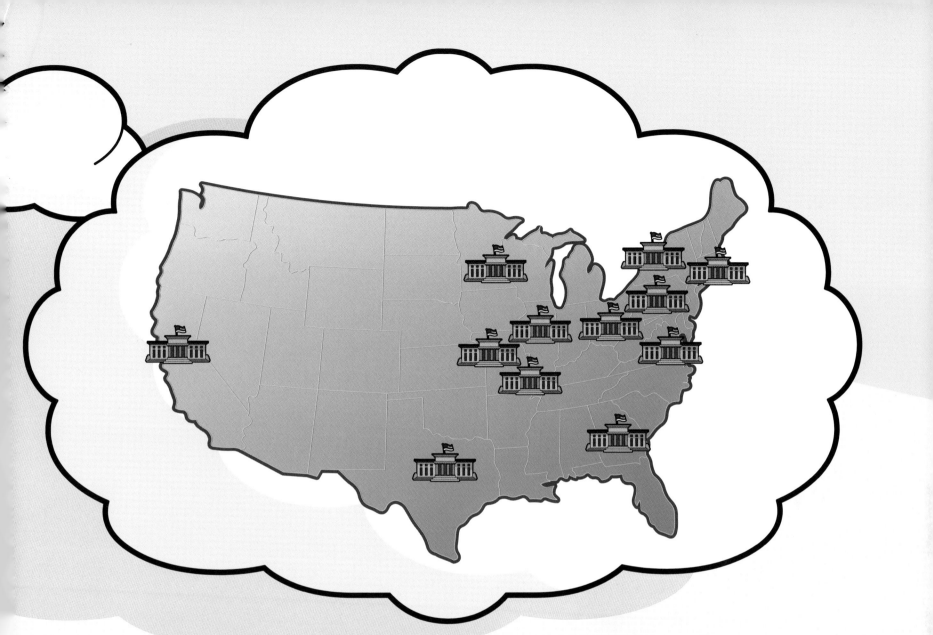

"The bank sends old bills to a special bank called the Federal Reserve Bank. The damaged bills and coins are destroyed, and we get new ones," Holly said. "There are 12 Federal Reserve Banks in the United States. Each one serves a different area. These banks are kind of like banks for banks. Even the government uses these banks."

Next, Mom showed David the bank's vault and the room with the safe-deposit boxes.

"The bank keeps its money in the vault," Mom said. "The vault is totally safe. It's even fireproof. See those boxes over there? Those are safe-deposit boxes. People rent the boxes to store valuable things like jewelry or legal papers," Mom told David.

SAFE-DEPOSIT BOXES

A safe-deposit box is very private and secure. No one can open the box without the renter's permission.

17

Next, Mom had an appointment with a man who wanted to borrow money to buy a new car. David watched while his mom looked over the loan application papers and asked a few questions.

"Everything looks good," she said. "You should be getting your loan in a few days."

"Great!" he said.

After the man left, David asked, "Why do people need loans?"

"Well, most people don't have enough money to buy expensive things like cars and houses," his mom said. "Sometimes people need money to send their kids to college or to start a business."

Before making loans, banks look over a person's financial history. This includes how much money the person earns, how much debt the person has, how much the person owns, and if the person pays bills on time.

"I bet I know what you like the most about your job," David said.

"What?" Mom asked.

"Seeing how happy people are when you tell them they're going to get the money they need," David said.

"You're right," Mom said with a grin. "Want to know my next favorite thing? It's the cookies in the break room. Let's go!"

How Banks Make Money

On page 18, David's mom approved a car loan. When a bank loans a person money, it charges interest. The borrower ends up paying more than the actual loan. This is how a bank makes a profit.

If the bank loaned you $10,000 for a five-year loan and charged you 8 percent interest, the bank would make $4,693. Follow the chart and find out how much you end up paying the bank for borrowing money for five years.

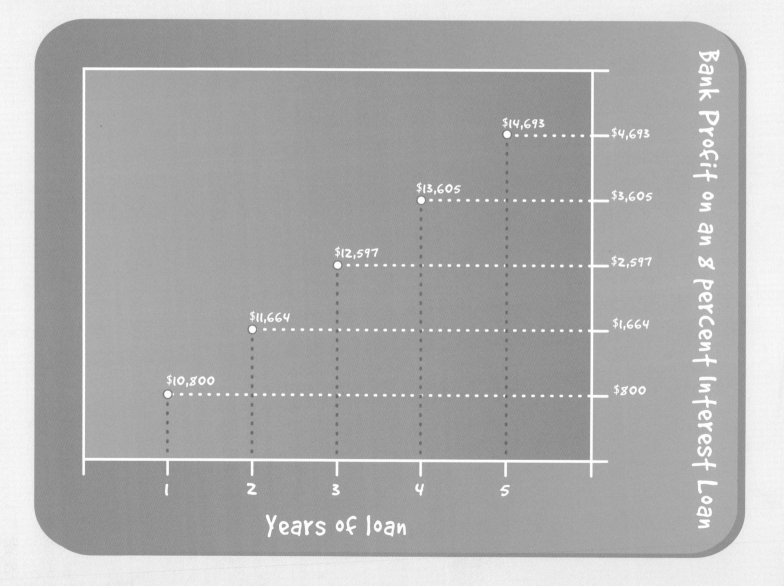

22

Fun Facts

- The average $1 bill lasts about 18-22 months.

- Interest is not the only way banks make a profit. Banks also charge small fees for some services.

- The headquarters of the Federal Reserve is in Washington, D.C.

- Old bills are sometimes recycled and turned into roofing shingles or insulation.

- A lot of banking transactions don't involve "real" money at all. EFT stands for electronic funds transfer. Money is transferred from one account to another over computer networks.

Glossary

ATM (automatic teller machine)—a machine that is connected to a large network of bank computers; it can dispense money and take deposits

debt—something that is owed

deposit—money added to an account

federal—the central government of the United States

financial—having to do with money

interest—the cost of borrowing money

loan—money that is borrowed with a plan to pay it back

Mesopotamia—an area in southwestern Asia between the Tigris and Euphrates rivers, in what is now Iraq

profit—money that a business makes after expenses have been subtracted

transaction—an exchange of money, goods, or services

withdrawal—money taken out of an account

23

TO LEARN MORE

At the Library

Giesecke, Ernestine. *Everyday Banking: Consumer Banking*. Chicago: Heinemann Library, 2002.

Leedy, Loreen. *Follow the Money!* New York: Holiday House, 2003.

Stone, L. *Keeping Money Safe*. Vero Beach, Florida: Rourke Publishing, 2003.

On the Web

FactHound offers a safe, fun way to find Web sites related to this book. All of the sites on FactHound have been researched by our staff.
www.facthound.com

1. Visit the FactHound home page.

2. Enter a search word related to this book, or type in this special code: 1404811567

3. Click on the FETCH IT button.

Your trusty FactHound will fetch the best sites for you!

Look for all of the books in the Money Matters series:

- Cash, Credit Cards, or Checks: A Book About Payment Methods
- In the Money: A Book About Banking
- Lemons and Lemonade: A Book About Supply and Demand
- Let's Trade: A Book About Bartering
- Save, Spend, or Donate? A Book About Managing Money
- Taxes, Taxes! Where the Money Goes
- Ups and Downs: A Book About the Stock Market
- That Costs Two Shells: The History of Money

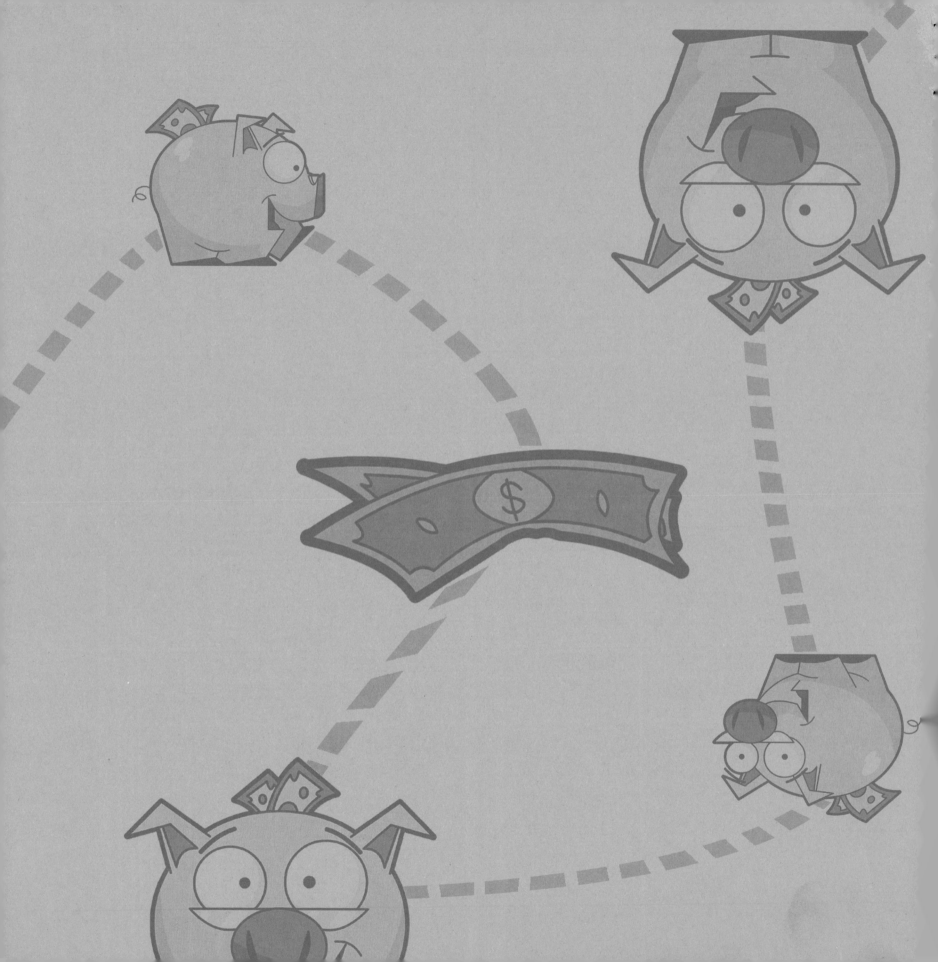